Copyright Law: Protecting Authors and Writers

By David K. Ewen, M.Ed.

Book 2 of the Professor Lecture Series

ISBN-13: 978-1535362481

ISBN-10: 1535362480

Copyright Law

Protecting Authors and Writers

Written by:

David K. Ewen, M.Ed.

Forest Academy

Ewen Prime Company

From the

Professor Lecture Series

About The Book

Copyright Law: Protecting Authors and Writers is based on an 11-year tour in the seven states of New York and New England that included copyright protection. The tour called the "Professor Lecture Series" included copyright law for publishing, broadcasting, filming, and content creation. A long-term veteran of book publishing, filming, and radio broadcasting, author David K. Ewen, M.Ed. has compiled the methodology that protects authors and writers from copyright infringement due to plagiarism. His experience simplifies necessary elements to put an author in possession of their manuscript prior to any possible plagiaristic interference. This formally puts an author's authenticated ownership prior to falsified plagiarism. David Ewen's legal experience in copyright law comes from nearly a quarter century of as a professional book publishing executive and noted expert.

About The Author

David K. Ewen, M.Ed. is an author, speaker, and talk show host on media topics related to digital multimedia technology, entrepreneurial studies, marketing, publicity, and business adventurism. He is the former Executive Director of the New England Publishers Association which was sold and re-founded as the Independent Publishers of New England. David toured the seven states of New England with his "Professor Lecture Series" for 11 years from 2004 to 2015.

Since 1998, David has been a radio talk show host, TV producer, filmmaker, and publicity event manager. This branch out to other media formats has made him a subject matter expert on digital multimedia technology.

As a touring professor, David K. Ewen, M.Ed. has lectured on a variety of media topics related to digital multimedia technology, entrepreneurial studies, marketing, publicity, and business adventurism.

Audiobook

The audiobook is part of the online Professor Lecture Series written and narrated by David K. Ewen, M.Ed. This content is an expanded version of what was presented during David's tour in the seven states of New York and New England from 2004 to 2015.

Preface

This content is composed of two parts. The first part is more of a testimony and memoir that explains my experience and copyright law as a book publisher. The second part talks about the three elements necessary to have in place to protect a writer or author from copyright infringement due to plagiarism in a court of law.

The purpose of presenting the first part representing a memoir is to give justification inauthenticity of the valid experience gained in copyright law as a book publisher. Without it, the second part which seem to have little credibility to the general community of writers and authors. This is not presented in a prideful or boastful way. There is no pride or anything to boast about. Very humbly, I am presenting the facts of experience that authenticates my explanation of copyright law to protect writers and authors.

I find the mistake that many authors and writers may as they feel that it is necessary to spend a lot of money related to copyright protection of their content. That simply isn't true. What is true is that the author needs to know what is necessary to protect themselves from copyright infringement due to plagiarism and what to do in the event that happens.

The mistake that many authors and writers make is that they think their content is safe from copyright infringement and plagiarism. That mistake is due to inexperience and ignorance. That is unfortunate and that is why there are so many victims.

My goal in presenting this content is to, first, validate my experience and then to, second, use my experience to protect writers and authors from copyright infringement. The historical importance of the memoir portion of this content also provide revelation of experience that writers and authors can use for improved understanding of copyright law.

So let's take a moment to explore a memoir of nearly a quarter century as a publisher and then later we will apply it to the practical application that protects authors from copyright infringement due to plagiarism.

Intent of Copyright

The intent of copyright protection is to place the authenticated writer or author in possession of their manuscript before any plagiarist attempts to stake claim to the content. This is done through a statement of clarity and a process that builds protection prior to any potential plagiarist activity. It may sound simple, but it is not. The common mistake authors and writers make is to skip

David K. Ewen, M.Ed.
"Professor Lecture Series"

necessary steps needed to protect themselves

against a plagiarist in a court of law.

David K. Ewen, M.Ed.
"Professor Lecture Series"

Part One …

Memoir of

Copyright

Experience

&

Overview

The Beginning

It was in 1994 when I launched my publishing company, Ewen Prime Company that began my work and copyright law. I never planned to become a lawyer and ever became a lawyer, however when one is intimately involved in book publishing, they are by default copyright law professionals. Anyone involved in book publishing working with writers, editors, and illustrators for more than two decades will be, by default, an expert in copyright law because of the nature of the work. This was proven evident during my 11-year tour called the Professor Lecture Series where I met prominent lawyers in New York, Connecticut, and Boston who agreed with my presentation of copyright law. They're pleased looks on their faces demonstrated that my experience in book publishing forced me to fully understand all facets of copyright law that are relevant to the author and the protection against copyright infringement due to plagiarism.

Authors work passionately on their written work which is an outpouring from their work. It is always a terrible shame when an author becomes a victim of copyright infringement due to plagiarism. I've seen it too often in more than 20 years during my publishing career. My publishing company, Ewen Prime Company, has brought on board many authors over the years and I made it my job to not only protect my office but also my publishing company. It was an absolute necessity. To do publishing correctly, you must by default do the process of copyright correctly. I call it a process because there are steps that are necessary before a

book is released into the market. There is no way

to go back in time to protect an author if the process

of copyright protection does not precede the release

of the book into the market. It is too late by that

time. A lack of planning and preparation that is

necessary, results with outcomes that are due to a

lack of planning and preparation. It's obvious and

simple. A bad effort in is a bad effort out.

Many authors and writers have missed important

steps in protecting their work and have approached

me when they have become victims of copyright infringement due to plagiarism. Some have approached me for help after the damage was done. There was nothing I could do given the fact that the authors had no mechanism in place that could be used in a court of law to prove themselves as the rightful owners of their content. The authenticity was not documented and recorded. That being said, there was no ammunition that could be used in a court of law that would enable a plaintiff to be successful.

David K. Ewen, M.Ed.
"Professor Lecture Series"

During my lectures at colleges and universities throughout the seven states of New York and New England from 2004 to 2015, I lectured on the topic of copyright law in the beginning of my presentation of book publishing, CD recording, TV production, and filmmaking. Most of the 18 lecture-topics that I offered during my tour involved a complete discussion of copyright law. It's such an important topic to discuss as one of the first agenda items in my lectures.

White lecturing on the topic of copyright law, I came across lawyers, paralegals, legal assistants, and even one TV actor who played a judge on the television show. Over the years, these individuals would challenge me with questions and find that my approach of copyright law followed the letter of the law and was as tight as a drum. They clearly saw that I had complete command of copyright law without formally being a lawyer myself.

It is absolutely necessary for anyone who calls themselves a book publisher who runs such an organization to completely understanding of copyright protection. they must also be fully aware of what element are protected and what can be shared. They must know the difference between copyright protected material and content that falls under the Creative Commons license.

Many people make the mistake thinking that just because they have a little C with a circle around it that they are protected under copyright law. In my lectures while traveling 25,000 miles over 11 years, I found this to be the most common mistake. The most disturbing thing that I found about the common knowledge of copyright is that people's understanding and misinterpretation of the copyright notice at the front of a book is all that they need to protect themselves in a court of law.

What authors and writers need to protect themselves against copyright infringement due to plagiarism requires up front steps completed prior to the release of their content into the market.   A mechanism needs to be put in place that put without a doubt the author in possession of the manuscript at a time before the defendant in such a case make claim of ownership. The mechanism is the formal documentation and recording of a form of witness, evidence, and date time stamp. A judge in a court of law wants to know of witnesses, exhibits, and a sequence of events. Actual courtroom experience and various forms of television representation of courtroom activity show this all the time.

The Author as Victim

An author becomes a victim of plagiarism when copyright infringement occurs against the work that they have published. When an author publishes work that is known not to be public domain and another party takes that work and publishes it as their own, then that constitutes copyright infringement and is plagiarism. The rights of the author, in such an example, is a violation of copyright law. The author is a victim of copyright infringement to plagiarism. The feeling in the victim's heart as an author is devastating because the author has had their personal contribution violated with no respect.

During my 11 years touring the seven states of New York and New England, I have asked my audience what it is like to have something stolen from them. the common theme that comes up is related to the word violation. This is true also for authors who suffer and have been victimized by copyright infringement due to plagiarism.   They all know about plagiarism, but think it will not happen to them. When it does, they feel violated.

In one of my lectures, a husband and a wife attended and share their story of a time when they were victims of copyright infringement do the plagiarism. The thief was the best man at their wedding. Imagine that. The best man at their wedding. Over the years I have heard all of the horror stories.

This severity of plagiarism and copyright infringement against an author's none-public-domain work is significant enough that I have chosen to discuss copyright law at the beginning of my lectures for 11 years during 2004 to 2015 when I toured the seven states of New York and New England conducting the Professor Lecture Series. I spoke about this topic for publishing, film production, CD recording, TV broadcasting, journalism, blogging, and more.

As a publisher and an author myself, I have put great effort into understanding copyright law and have become a subject matter expert after nearly a quarter of a century in business. I take protecting proprietary license of content seriously.

David K. Ewen, M.Ed.
"Professor Lecture Series"

Copyright Page

Nearly every book that has been formally published has a copyright page that includes the standard copyright notice indicating ownership of content and that all rights are reserved to that owner. In my lectures, I help people understand the significance of what the copyright notice is and that in no way is it identified as the only tool to protect an author or writer in a court of law.

The copyright law is only a statement of fact that needs to be supported by other elements outside of what is seen in the written published book to serve as protection of copyright in a court of law.

Let me use an example of the statement of fact that a copyright notice offers. Dr. Edgar Mitchell was the sixth man to walk on the Moon during the Apollo era of spaceflight. He was on my radio show and we discussed briefly his experience in space and his travel to another celestial body. He is part of a small club of people who are recognized as having accomplished this feat. There are pictures of Dr. Edgar Mitchell that show him saluting the American flag on the Moon. Does this mean Dr. Mitchell own the Moon? Does this mean he owns the Moon in the same way he owns his house on earth? No this does not mean that. The flag on the Moon is a stake to claim. The claim is that the United States arrived first to the Moon in a manned exploration voyage. Will other countries accomplish the same thing? Of course they will, but when they do they will be able to say that they are second and not first. They will not be able to make the claim that they were first. There is evidence of that with the planting of the American flag on the surface of the Moon that has for decades.

Just like the flag on the Moon, the copyright statement in a book is a stake a claim. It is the statement that the book is not public domain and that there is a designated owner of the content. Does that alone protect the author in a court of law in the event that they become a victim of copyright infringement due to plagiarism? Of course not. All the copyright notice does is make this statement

David K. Ewen, M.Ed.
"Professor Lecture Series"

that the content is not public domain. In the event that the defendant in a court case related to plagiarism is found guilty, then it is known and affirmed by the copyright notice that when plagiarism took place it was done knowingly and deliberately. The copyright notice prevents the defendant from saying in a court of law that they did not know that the work was not public domain.

The best ways to show the critical elements necessary for copyright protection is to go back to your own jury duty experience, courtroom reality TV shows, and television dramas that include courtroom experiences. My personal favorite is the courtroom reality TV shows that are designed in such a way to have the judge come down hard on the defendant when their defense is so weak and limited. Some of those scenes are so funny to watch.

In any courtroom scenario, whether it be on television or in reality, a piece of paper that makes a statement is not sufficient. An example is the copyright page found in a book. That has some degree of importance but means nothing alone and by itself. The copyright notice page is only a statement and in no way act as an enforcer. A statement is in no way considered copyright protection. The protection comes from a process completed upfront prior to the release of content to the market. This process is most often missed resulting in authors and writers losing copyright battles in a court of law because of insufficient evidence. Either in person or on television, you always see the plaintiff and defendant have a discussion on witnesses, evidence, and time frame. The process involving copyright protection in a court of law relates to compiling those three elements in advance and in such a way that they are were the exhibits in a court of law. Authors and writers who have not been stung by plagiarism before or are new to the industry often think that these steps are not necessary. They make the mistake of believing that becoming a victim of copyright infringement to the plagiarism is of low risk. That is a terrible mistake to make.

The only thing that a copyright notice in a book says is that the content is not public domain. Nothing more. It is just a statement and notification. Overall it has little relevance to the tangible protection necessary for an author or writer in a court of law.

If someone were to be found plagiarizing the content of another, their defense maybe that they thought it was public domain. As silly as it may sound, that can work in court if the copyright notice is not properly displayed. A person can issue a lawsuit for spilling hot coffee on themselves and win large sums of money. That happened. Again, it is silly, but a stake to claim is necessary for what may seem as obvious.

All the copyright notice page of a book does is to make the state to claim that the work is not public domain. Anything that is considered public domain is freely available to the public to use in any way they want. Public domain content is open content that is considered open to the market and free for use in any fashion.

The plagiarist has the opportunity to falsely claim
that the plagiarized content is theirs and that they
originated it. They can offer a counterclaim that the
original author is actually the plagiarist. Can the
original author prove that to be false in a court of
law? Are they ready? Did they make the
preparations in advance that proves their own
authenticity as the originating author? A printed
copyright notice is not enough. The question comes
into play that relates to authenticity of the author
and the authenticity of the timeline indicating

origination. This physical evidence created in advance is what is admissible in a court of law. The actual physical contents would then be compared with origination and recent publication to see if they match shows sufficient evidence of plagiarism.

Public Domain

Let's have a clear understanding of what public domain means. Public domain is not defined as content that can in any way be considered copyrighted. There is no copyright protection for content that is identified and designated as public domain. This type of contents is free and open to the public to use in any fashion that they desire without infringing on any copyright protection. In some cases, content that is identified as public domain may not even have an original author identified.

A book that has a copyright page with the standard copyright notice is making the state to claim that the contents of the book is in no way to be considered public domain.   That copyright page alone does not protect the author in a court of law. The only thing a copyright notice page does is to serve as an identifier or a flag that indicates that the contents of the book is not public domain.

In the event an author is a victim of copyright infringement to the plagiarism, then much more physical tangible evidence admissible in court is necessary to be available and used in a court of law to protect their rights as copyright owner. Plagiarism is identified as an infringement of an author's right as copyright owner of content. Quite simply it is stealing, robbery, and the actions of a thief. It is an illegal violation of the proprietary rights of an owner. To the author, it is a very hurtful violation.

Creative Commons License

There are few people that know what a Creative Commons license is and even fewer people that know the difference of that and public domain. Content that has a Creative Commons license compared to public domain content is totally different as it pertains to the copyright arena. The mistake most people make is that Creative Commons license is the same as public domain. It is not.

Content that has a Creative Commons license is one that has copyright protection, however given freely by the author to the public for the purposes of building upon their work. In this case, content can be used, but with recognition of the author owning the content with the Creative Commons license. This type of content has an owner associated with it. Contents associated with public domain most often does not. Creative Commons and Public Domain are not the same.

It is easy to find contents under the Creative Commons license voice searching for Creative Commons media on the internet. this type of content is clearly identified as being under the Creative Commons license that authorizes others to use the content.

Symbols of Protection

The written symbols of protection is different for copyright, public domain, and creative commons. A copyright notice uses the small C with a circle around it ©. Public domain is recognized by the copyright notice with a forward slash crossing through the letter C. Another representation of public domain is the letters PD with a circle around it. the Creative Commons license for content is identified with a CC with a circle around it. It

looks like the copyright symbol but with 2 letter Cs'
with a circle around it.

Normally, the copyright symbol has other standardized text that goes along with it. For example, Copyright © 2016, "Author", All Rights Reserved. The phrase, "All Rights Reserved" means that the right of content ownership is reserved to the author and no one else,

David K. Ewen, M.Ed.
"Professor Lecture Series"

Part 2 …
Copyright
Process

Legal Elements of Protection

The legal elements of protection that are used in a court of law are designed for the plaintiff to properly identify infringement by the defendant with documented evidence reviewed by the judge or jury. Most often, copyright legal cases are corporate in nature and do not have a jury. These types of cases are decided by the judge who is well-versed in copyright law.

David K. Ewen, M.Ed.
"Professor Lecture Series"

Although they may not know it, the general public

has observed the legal elements of protection used

in a court of law even on television with courtroom

reality TV and television shows that include

courtroom drama. These elements are also seen

when a person satisfies their jury duty obligation as

a United States citizen.

The benefits of knowing the legal elements of

protection used in copyright law is that it helps to

understand what happens in a courtroom between

the plaintiff defendant and judge. The beautiful

thing about copyright law is it helps to understand

ways of legal protection and fighting for legal rights

in areas beyond copyright law. In nearly a quarter

of a century working with copyright law, I have

come in contact with lawyers and legal

professionals and have shared my copyright law

experience that was found to be receptive and

compliant within the legal community.

Industry Understanding

During a lecture at a community college, a legal professional who was in attendance had disagreed with my presentation of how authors can be protected against infringement due to plagiarism. In my introduction at the early stages of my copyright section of the lecture a prominent legal professionals stood up and disagreed with me. At the time I did not know they were a prominent legal professional that was well-known in the area. I did not live in the area, so I had no way of knowing who this person was or their credentials. As I continued speaking, other legal professionals attending the lecture asked the first legal professional to sit down. I asked a legal professional to stand up and then, when I finished, I told him to sit down. A round of applause followed and the prominent legal who was disruptive to the lecture was embarrassed as he was wrong. My goal and intent was not to embarrass anyone. I do not do that. however, the number of years and publishing commands authority in copyright law. In agreement with others in attendance, that authority was valid and given proof. The very nature of book publishing results fin commanding authority of copyright law as it pertains to the courtroom arena.

This story is not one of pride or intended to be boastful in nature.   Experience commands legitimate authority.   This story is a demonstration of what actually happened.   It taught me something.   I didn't have to be an overpriced lawyer in a pinstriped suit with all kinds of degrees to help authors protect their content ownership in a court of law. Solid book publishing experience as an executive and subject matter expert in the industry proves is a valid substitute to passing lawyer examinations. Doing anything for nearly a quarter of a century will make one a professional qualified subject matter expert. This story demonstrated that to be true.

In another year, in the Boston area, a very experienced lawyer explained that he was impressed with the way the legal process was explained in my lecture. He thought I was a lawyer. I explained to him that passionate book publishers by default are forced into being well-versed in copyright law methodologies. Again, over two decades and book publishing will do that.

These are just two examples among many that occurred in the seven states of New York and New England during the 11-year tour of the Professor Lecture Series from July 2004 to August 2015. The lecture reached a total of 52 venues that were part of the tour with frequent events occurring multiple times each week. Tough questions were asked and logic and understanding was provided as answers.

This experience has shown me that nearly a quarter of a century in copyright law is sufficient. As mentioned before in my introduction, anyone in book publishing who has the need to protect authors from plagiarism and copyright infringement must, absolutely understand how to protect authors in a court of law. There is no exception. It is the job of the publisher of books or any other type of media to have an understanding of copyright law and how protection in a courtroom plays out.

More importantly then what happens in the courtroom, it is necessary to follow the necessary steps and procedures that prepare for any potential courtroom activity. The success in the courtroom is based on the success that occurs before going into the courtroom. The idea is to prevent the courtroom experience.

Personal Legal Drama

In my early years has a publisher, when I hired editors, writers, and illustrators, I had all freelance staff sign contracts indicating that the publisher of the content that was created. Their honorarium or stipend would either be unidentified flat rate or it would be 50% of the sales no matter how big or small.

One of my authors who wrote a book of poetry had signed a contract indicating that the publisher on the content and that the author would be paid 50% of the sales no matter how big or small. There were absolutely no fees that the author had to pay. And understanding in the contract indicated that the publisher owned the content because they were paying for it to be marketed and distributed and sold. This author accepted the agreement and signed the contract.

The sale of the book was not successful. The author was unhappy that the book did not sell well and reacted by hiring lawyers with the intent to cause harm rather than be compensated for damages. There were no damages suffered by the author. His emotional reaction caused an action that was not warranted.

The goal of the author was to have my publishing company shut down in ownership of the content returned to him. All of this activity would be intended to be done out of court. He hired lawyers who in turn, put the author's request in writing and sent it to me. The legal statement came from the author with the backing of the lawyers, but not with the lawyer's understanding of what the author was doing. This occurred in the late 1990s so the idea of email was relatively new as compared to the way email is used today. The authors legal team would email me statements and comments and directives. I would print off the email and mail it back to the law office with multiple corrections indicating poor grammar and sentence structure. After multiple times of going through this process of embarrassing the author's legal team's knowledge of grammar and sentence structure, I thought it best to make a phone call in end this situation.

When I called the law office representing the author, they explained to me that the author said I was an employee of the author. I shared the contract and proved that the author was an employee of the publishing company as a freelancer with content provided being owned by the publishing company. I also said that I was comfortable with returning all rights to the author even though it was not required for me to do so. I reported that I was giving the rights to the author only as a kind courtesy.

The legal professional that I was speaking with on the phone who was representing the author was embarrassed and realized what the author was trying to do. The intent of the author was to have me sign documentation that would in effect shut my company down even though it was not related to the book he wrote. The legal professional representing the author finally saw that the author was frustrated that the book that he wrote did not sell.

The legal professional asked me why I accepted taking this client knowing that he may have had personal issues of self-confidence and anger. I explained that the author was a friend of one of my family members and I was being helpful and courteous in ways that went beyond normal expectation. It is my nature to give respect and be helpful. That author took advantage of that. Again, the legal professional was embarrassed.

The legal case that the author had put forth against me was dropped by the author's own lawyers. The primary reason why the case was dropped was due to embarrassment.   The legal team relied on documentation provided by the author that would be forwarded to me.   They made the mistake of trusting the author without analysis.   Their own client made fools out of them. the legal documentation of which the lawyers had sent me to sign came originally from the author which was littered with the medical errors and sentence structure mistakes. The law office saw that I was investing time and cost to print off these documents from email and send by regular mail with corrections. I wonder how much the author paid the lawyers for that waste of time. I wonder what the author learned after paying the bill for his lawyers.

This taught me that even people who are in your inner circles within your own organization may turn their back on you. I do not share this to tell people to be afraid of the team that they work with.

I share this story to let others know that the contracts that I had all of my editors, illustrators, and writers sign before working with me is important. There is the expression that says if it isn't written, then it wasn't said. I am clear up front to responsibilities, expectations, consequences, ownership, licenses, and more.

I remember one time having a conversation with an assistant vice-president of a prominent investment firm in Boston who asked me the question if I had a lawyer create my contract. I did not. I was well-versed in copyright law in the process of legal protection. I was organized and structured in the way that I handled legal matters. There is that expression that says if it hasn't been written it wasn't said. If an opportunity to exist for two sides of a controversy to arise, then it is necessary to put in place legal protection. That is done in writing. If you have ever seen lawyers work in an office or in a courtroom, be it on TV or in person, you may have noticed that they carry a flutter of papers in their briefcases and bags.

Documentation is absolutely necessary for any level of legal protection. Written documents are what defines the law. An example is the Declaration of Independence and the Bill of Rights that formed the United States of America.

What you have experienced so far was the memoir part of this content. Let's now go to the next part that describes the copyright process. A statement of copyright alone will not protect from copyright infringement due to plagiarism. Although that is very important, there is a lot more necessary.

To protect from copyright infringement due to plagiarism, there is a process that must be followed. Certain steps must be completed prior to the release of content into the market. These steps are the ammunition needed to serve as plaintiff in the event copyright ownership must be proven.

Three Elements of Law

There are three elements associated with the discussion between a plaintiff and a defendant. This is true in any courtroom situation. Anything outside of those three elements will cause the judge to have that information strike from the record. Those three elements are witness, evidence, and date and time stamp. The judge wants to know who else was there who can vouch for what happened, what do you have to show the judge as an exhibit, and in what order and time did the sequence of events happen.   In short, the judge

will ask you when your witness saw what you did.

Again it goes back to witness, evidence, and date

and time stamp.   Knowing this in advance is very

helpful to have legal preparation prepared before

going to a courtroom should the need arise.   That

being said, it is necessary to have those three

elements in place that is relevant to contents that an

author is trying to protect.

Take a moment and think about the courtroom

drama seen on TV and court reality TV shows that

you have seen before. Have you noticed that the judge focuses solely on authenticity through witness, documentation for evidence, and attention to when things occurred? Have you also noticed that the side that wins the case is the one that has the witness authenticity, the documented evidence, and a clear understanding of when things occurred? This is because the winning side is prepared and organized. They also know what it takes to win a case.

An author wanting to protect their content must have witnessed authenticity, documented evidence, and a record of when things occurred. The integration of these three elements is what helps protect an author in a court of law in the event they are a victim of plagiarism and copyright infringement occurs.

Poor Man's Copyright

At first glance, would I describe may sound like a poor man's copyright. Without following the instructions properly, then it is a poor man's copyright. That is because it is done wrong. The process of copyright protection that I described for authors and content developers is not a poor man's copyright. Although it involves mailing contents yourself, there are many steps that must be done in order for it to be done correctly. When steps are missed then the process of copyright protection will not work in a court of law. The difference between what I share as a copyright process is very much different than a poor man's copyright.

The story that I shared before that occurred in New York when a prominent legal professional disagreed with what I was presenting is related to his understanding that I was discussing the poor man's copyright. His early assumption missed the importance of important key steps that is necessary for the process of copyright to be effective in preparing an author in a court of law.

Taking a shortcut or having an omission of any of the steps that I provide in the copyright process is a poor man's copyright because it is done wrong. Because time will be taken to manage the copyright process, it is in the best interest for the author to complete the process correctly. This is something that should not be taken lightly or be glossed over. Many authors make the mistake of doing that and lose in a copyright battle in court. A lack of seriousness in copyright protection results in a lack of seriousness from the judge for your defense.

Don't make the mistake of skipping over important

steps.

Explaining Three Elements

As mentioned before, there are three elements necessary to protect an author when they become a victim of plagiarism due to copyright infringement. My explanation will involve discussing each element independently followed by combining all elements together. It is important to note that each element is important however not sufficient when operating alone. However, each element will be discussed independently for clarity and understanding. The elements discussed involve witness evidence and a date and time stamp. The witness demonstrates authenticity. The evidence is a form of documentation. And the date and time stamp is an accurate record of when things occurred. Each of those elements will be discussed in detail and then tied together. It is the timing of those elements together is what constitutes the protection and other has when they have become a victim of plagiarism due to copyright infringement.

The process being outlined is to provide an exhibit that is admissible in a court of law documenting that an author was in possession of a manuscript at an authenticated and verified point in time. The three elements are related to specifically the author, the manuscript, and the origination of possession. The three key pieces will involve a notarized letter, the manuscript as evidence, and the proper use of an envelope.

Some people may think that I'm referring to what is called the poor man's copyright where the manuscript is mailed to themselves. I present something similar, but with important differences.

What they are referring to is called the poor man's copyright because what they are doing is wrong and ineffective. It is sloppy. Of course it is what they say it is. They need to change to the correct methodology.

Witness

The purpose of the witnesses to authenticate that the author is who they say they are. There is nothing more to it. The easiest way to do that is to have a simple letter notarized. When a person goes to a notary they need to show a valid government-issued ID such as a driver's license or passport that authenticate the owner's identity. This notarized letter can be very simple and does not need to have a lot written on it. It is suggested that the letter be a simple statement of the author's name and their relation to the title of the book being published.

The process of getting a letter notarized involves a certified person who is recognized as an official notary who document their client's identity by validating an ID and stamping a document. That document is then signed by the notary and then embossed with a seal.

This simple letter that is authenticated by a notary is an official document that clearly identifies that the author says who they are. The notarized letter

represents the author in a documented form. It is

important that you recognize this. A notarized

letter is a way of putting on paper the authenticity

of who someone is. That document is a paper

version of the author because a witness has formally

documented it through notarization. This is a key

element that many authors and writers forget when

going through the copyright process. There are

other elements they forget, but this is one of the

important ones. Again, missed steps results in a

poor-man's copyright due to being done wrong.

David K. Ewen, M.Ed.
"Professor Lecture Series"

Evidence

The evidence is the manuscript that is owned by the author. some people have asked me if a digital form of the manuscript can be used as evidence instead of a printed document. Digital media formats have changed over the years. It is best to use paper. In a court of law that is what you see legal professionals use. To save on printing costs, the printing parameters can be set such that four pages of the manuscript are printed on one standard letter size

paper.   This way for 100 Pages worth of

manuscript only 25 pages are physically printed.

As an added layer of legal protection, it is okay to

have the same document saved on a flash drive or

CD.

Envelope

The next step is to place in a package envelope the notarized letter and the manuscript. The envelope should be sealed. That envelope is now a time capsule. Think of what is inside that envelope. That envelope contains elements of witness and evidence. Although the notarized letter may have a date on it, that is not the date and time stamp that will be referring to as part of the copyright process being discussed.

If the notarized letter represents the author in the manuscript represents the evidence, then the envelope represent possession. The author and the evidence are kept together by way of the envelope which interns shows that the author was in possession of the evidence.   This is further proven when the package is sealed.

US Post Office.

The envelope is brought to the United States Post Office and it is sent to your home address. It must be certified and with return receipt. It is important that this package envelope be mailed to your home address certified and with return receipt. It is also important to note that the United States Post Office that is used is the one that is local to your home address. The idea is if you are to sign this package that is certified and with return receipt, it will never leave the building. This way there is no condition where the package gets lost in the mail.   It never leaves the building.

Let's say, for example, that you bring this package envelope to the United States Post Office and mail it to yourself certified and return receipt on a Monday. On Tuesday you will receive in the mail that you have a package to sign for at the post office. on that same day you go to the post office and sign for the package. On Wednesday, you receive the green return receipt postcard in the mail.

You take that green return receipt postcard and put it with the package. At no time do you open the package. The package must have remained closed and sealed for it to be admissible in a court of law.

After receiving the green return receipt postcard, go to the United States post office website and print off the tracking information that is represented on both the green return receipt postcard and the package.

Date and Time Stamp

We have already talked about witness and evidence which are the notarized letter and the manuscript that is sealed in the envelope that was sent to yourself via certified and return receipt at the United States Post Office. The final element needed in a court of law is the date and time stamp. This was produced with the certified and return receipt at the United States Post Office. The green receipt postcard with a barcode on it matches the barcode on the package. That tracking information represented by the barcode can be printed from the United States Post Office website.

It is important to note that the United States Post Office is a United States government agency. It is a federal office. Any action associated with sending or receiving certified and return receipt packages is done inside a federal government building. It may not be the fanciest building around however it is still a federal government building.

The printing on the package, on the green return receipt postcard, the barcodes provided, and the tracking information printed from the United States post office website is the date and time stamp needed as the final element that an author uses in a court of law.

Three Elements Prepared

The completion of the copyright process should have a notarized letter with a manuscript inside a sealed envelope that was mailed to you or cell certified and return receipt. The witness is the notarized letter that authenticates the author is who they say they are. The evidence is the manuscript that is sealed inside an envelope with the notarized letter. The date and time stamp is represented by the labeling on the package and the historical information provided by the United States Post Office.

Because the envelope is sealed the date the package was sent is the date that the notarized letter that identifies the author was next to the evidence that identifies the manuscript.

The notarized letter represents the author. the envelope represents possession. The manuscript represents property. All three elements show that the author was in possession of the manuscript on a specific date. That specific date is win the certified package was sent return receipt and documented by the tracking information printed from the United States post office website.

It is important to repeat that's a notarized letter represents the author through authenticity. the manuscript represents the property being claimed by the author. the envelope represents possession that puts the author in the manuscript together. The package shows that the author was in possession of the manuscript on a specific date which is represented by the records proving and

documented by the United States Post Office which

is a federal government agency.

Second Package

In the event an author who is a victim of plagiarism due to copyright infringement needs to see a lawyer then two packages instead of one are necessary. One is for the lawyer and the other is for the judge. Both remain unopened. The lawyer will open their package before the judge does. The judge must open their own package for review as an exhibit in a court of law.

A lawyer needs to see the preparation and author has put in place that proves copyright infringement. this involves opening the package that was described previously for the copyright process. If the lawyer representing the author brings the open package to a judge, then the judge will say the evidence is tampered and not admissible in a court of law.

It is important that both the lawyer for the author in the judge receive the unopened, package that represents, witness evidence and date and time stamp. the copyright process for two packages can be done at once rather than one after the other. For example, instead of having one letter brought to the notary for signature and validation, there can be true. When the author goes to the United States Post Office to send the package certified and return receipt there can be two packages sent instead of one. the end result is that the lawyer has what they need to accept the case and the judge has what they need to process the case.

The idea of having two packages instead of one is not known by many people. It is important that when being represented by legal counsel that they have all of the resources including an additional an open to admit as evidence as an exhibit for the prosecution.

Summary of Process

The process of copyright protection for authors involves witness evidence and date and time stamp. The witness is represented by a notarized letter. The evidence is represented by the manuscript. The date and time stamp is represented by the records shown of the notarized letter and manuscripts sealed in an envelope mailed certified and return receipt to the author. A total of two identical packages are sent to the author which are identical. One is for the author's legal counsel and the other is for the judge

to determine verdict.

In a court of law, the author who is a victim of

plagiarism due to copyright infringement is the

plaintiff and the opposing the party who allegedly

committed the crime of plagiarism is the defendant.

Damages Awarded

One of the things that they don't tell you in law
school is that the plaintiff may allow the defendant
to benefit financially so that the awarded judgement
to the plaintiff can be greater.   An author who is
victim of plagiarism due to copyright infringement
will observe the plagiarist Revenue rise. when that
Revenue growth plateaus and levels off, it is then
that the originating author who is a victim of
plagiarism due to copyright infringement files a suit

against the alleged plagiarist. The winning of a case would then result at a higher awarded judgement as the damages are identified by the revenue gained by the plagiarist.

The damages awarded to the plaintiff is in relation to the revenue generated by the defendant do to plagiaristic behavior. this is why some authors will not act immediately against a plagiarist if the revenue being generated is significant.

Conclusion

Although I have been working in copyright law for nearly a quarter of a century, I have never served as legal counsel to an author except those who were working for me as freelancers and we're under contract. Copyright law is such a unique niche-legal-genre that it is commonly more expensive than need be in terms of legal services with a lawyer. My hope is that my experience saves authors money that can be better served in their marketing efforts to get their books sold.

The important thing to remember is that copyright
protection involves the three elements of witness,
evidence, and a date-time stamp. All of these
elements are formally documented in tied together.
It shows that the author is placed with the
manuscript at a specific time in the past. It further
demonstrates that the author is in possession of the
manuscript at a specific time in the past. the
envelope represents possession and the notarized
letter represents the author. The manuscript

enclosed in the envelope along with the notarized

letter is the tangible evidence.

The Author's Future

When I started in book publishing back in 1994, the only media involved was a paper-based book.   That later expanded to ebooks with the evolution and revolution of the tablet computer. Because of the present-day iniquitousness of the mobile device. audiobooks have been given a second life and are now flourishing.   With digital multimedia content, Authors are now taking advantage of video-book-trailers that have the same Effectiveness as movie trailers.   With an increased number of channels to release content by the author, it is now increasingly more important that the author be aware of the copyright process.   The steps are called a process because it is a process that is necessary before the release of the book.

Steps of Copyright Process

Witness

Notarized letter

Evidence

Copy of Manuscript

Date/Time

Mail letter and manuscript in envelope to your address from a local post office. Mail certified and return receipt.

Exhibit for court (next page)

Exhibit for Court

The author is in possession of the manuscript on the day the package was sent. The notarized letter represents the author. The envelope represents possession. The records from the United States Post Office represents the authenticated verified timeline.

Final Words

The discussion of copyright in this content is related to a process to provide a mechanism to protect authors from copyright infringement in the event they are a victim of plagiarism. It is a respected process that works.

For more information with greater drilled down detail of copyright law beyond what was discussed here, the U.S. Copyright Office, located in Washington, D.C., has a public website:

www.copyright.gov

David K. Ewen, M.Ed.
"Professor Lecture Series"

Checklist

- Notarized Letter (2 copies)

- Copy of Manuscript (total two)

- Envelope   with   Notarized   Letter   and

  Manuscript (two envelopes)

- Go to local post office

- Send Envelope certified and return receipt

- Next day – Sign for package – Do not open

- Next day – Get return receipt card

- Print tracking information from USPS website

Copyright Law

Protecting Authors and Writers

Written by:

David K. Ewen, M.Ed.

Forest Academy

Ewen Prime Company

From the

Professor Lecture Series